HAL·LEONARD

WEDDING ESSENTIALS

INCLUDES REFERENCE CD

WORSHIP FOR WEDDINGS

ISBN 978-1-4234-8928-3

HAL·LEONARD®
CORPORATION

7777 W. BLUEMOUND RD. P.O. BOX 13819 MILWAUKEE, WI 53213

Visit Hal Leonard Online at
www.halleonard.com

WORSHIP FOR WEDDINGS

BE UNTO YOUR NAME

Words and Music by LYNN DeSHAZO
and GARY SADLER

CENTER

Words and Music by CHARLIE HALL
and MATT REDMAN

BROKEN AND BEAUTIFUL

Words and Music by BRIAN DOERKSEN
and JOSH FOX

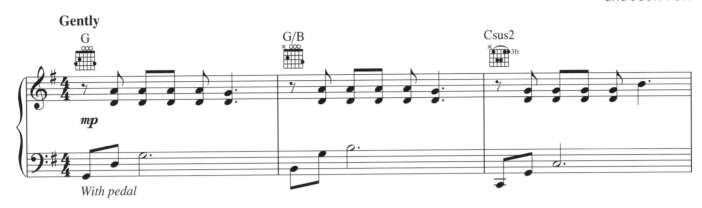

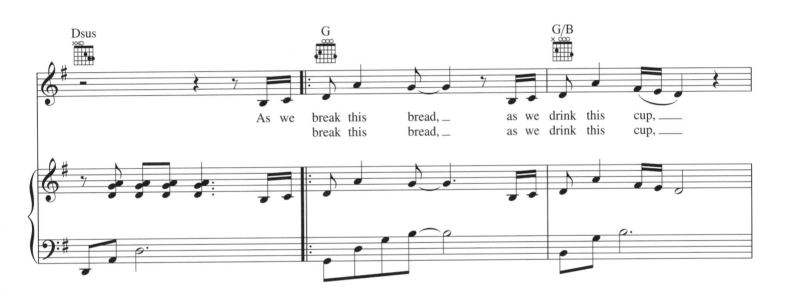

THE GIFT OF LOVE

Words by HAL H. HOPSON
English Melody adapted by HAL H. HOPSON

HOLY GROUND

Words and Music by
GERON DAVIS

HE IS HERE

Words and Music by PAUL BALOCHE
and BRIAN DOERKSEN

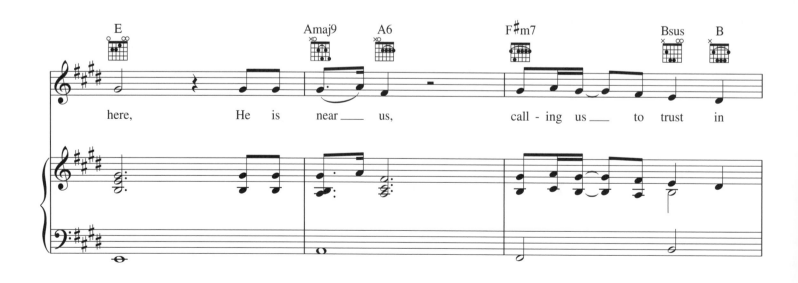

HERE AND NOW

Words and Music by PAUL BALOCHE
and BRENTON BROWN

HOW BEAUTIFUL

Words and Music by
TWILA PARIS

LISTEN TO OUR HEARTS

Words and Music by GEOFF MOORE
and STEVEN CURTIS CHAPMAN

TODAY
(As for Me and My House)

Words and Music by BRIAN DOERKSEN
and SANDRA GAGE

* Recorded a half step higher.

The Wedding Essentials series is a great resource for wedding musicians, featuring beautiful arrangements for a variety of instruments. Each book includes a reference CD to help couples choose the perfect songs for their wedding ceremony or reception.

Christian Wedding Favorites

Answered Prayer • God Causes All Things to Grow • God Knew That I Needed You • Household of Faith • I Will Be Here • If You Could See What I See • Love Will Be Our Home • Seekers of Your Heart • This Day • 'Til the End of Time.
00311941 P/V/G... $16.99

Contemporary Wedding Ballads

Beautiful in My Eyes • Bless the Broken Road • Endless Love • (Everything I Do) I Do It for You • From This Moment On • Have I Told You Lately • Here and Now • Love of a Lifetime • More Than Words • When You Say You Love Me.
00311942 P/V/G... $16.99

Love Songs for Weddings

Grow Old with Me • Here, There and Everywhere • If • Longer • Part of My Heart • Valentine • We've Only Just Begun • The Wedding Song • You and I • You Raise Me Up.
00311943 Piano Solo $16.99

Service Music for Weddings

PROCESSIONALS, RECESSIONALS, LIGHTING OF THE UNITY CANDLE
Allegro maestoso • Amazing Grace • Ave Maria • Canon in D • Jesu, Joy of Man's Desiring • Jupiter (Chorale Theme) • O Perfect Love • Ode to Joy • Rondeau • Trumpet Voluntary.
00311944 Piano Solo $14.99

Wedding Guitar Solos

All I Ask of You • Gabriel's Oboe • Grow Old with Me • Hallelujah • Here, There and Everywhere • More Than Words • Sunrise, Sunset • Wedding Song (There Is Love) • When I Fall in Love • You Raise Me Up.
00701335 Guitar Solo $16.99

Wedding Vocal Solos

Grow Old with Me • I Swear • In My Life • Longer • The Promise (I'll Never Say Goodbye) • Someone Like You • Sunrise, Sunset • Till There Was You • Time After Time • We've Only Just Begun.
00311945 High Voice.. $16.99
00311946 Low Voice $16.99

Worship for Weddings

Be Unto Your Name • Broken and Beautiful • Center • He Is Here • Here and Now • Holy Ground • How Beautiful • Listen to Our Hearts • Today (As for Me and My House).
00311949 P/V/G... $16.99

FOR MORE INFORMATION, SEE YOUR LOCAL MUSIC DEALER, OR WRITE TO:

HAL•LEONARD®
CORPORATION
7777 W. BLUEMOUND RD. P.O. BOX 13819 MILWAUKEE, WI 53213

www.halleonard.com

Prices, content, and availability subject to change without notice.

The Best
PRAISE & WORSHIP
Songbooks for Piano

Above All
THE PHILLIP KEVEREN SERIES
15 beautiful praise song piano solo arrangements by Phillip Keveren. Includes: Above All • Agnus Dei • Breathe • Draw Me Close • He Is Exalted • I Stand in Awe • Step by Step • We Fall Down • You Are My King (Amazing Love) • and more.
00311024 Piano Solo...................................$11.95

The Best Praise & Worship Songs Ever
80 all-time favorites: Awesome God • Breathe • Days of Elijah • Here I Am to Worship • I Could Sing of Your Love Forever • Open the Eyes of My Heart • Shout to the Lord • We Bow Down • dozens more.
00311057 P/V/G $19.95

Modern Hymns
NEW CLASSICS FOR TODAY'S WORSHIPPER
Piano/vocal/guitar arrangements of 20 worship favorites: Amazing Grace (My Chains Are Gone) • How Deep the Father's Love for Us • In Christ Alone • Take My Life • The Wonderful Cross • and more.
00311739 P/V/G $14.95

More of the Best Praise & Worship Songs Ever
76 more contemporary worship favorites, including: Beautiful One • Everlasting God • Friend of God • How Great Is Our God • In Christ Alone • Let It Rise • Mighty to Save • Your Grace Is Enough • more.
00311800 P/V/G $24.99

Everlasting God
Our matching folio includes: Beautiful One • Everlasting God • Holy Is the Lord • Hosanna • In Christ Alone • Lord, Reign in Me • We Fall Down • You Never Let Go • and more.
00311790 P/V/G $14.95

51 Must-Have Modern Worship Hits
A great collection of 51 of today's most popular worship songs, including: Amazed • Better Is One Day • Everyday • Forever • God of Wonders • He Reigns • How Great Is Our God • Offering • Sing to the King • You Are Good • and more.
00311428 P/V/G $19.95

Piano Interludes for Worship
by David Ritter
This songbook is designed to offer musical support and a soothing ambiance for various aspects of the worship service, such as Communion, Prayer, Scripture Reading, Invitation, etc. 14 original pieces, including: Ambiance • Consecration • Devotion • Passion • Pensive • Reflection • Sanctus • and more.
00311472 Piano Solo....................................$9.95

Praise & Worship Duets
THE PHILLIP KEVEREN SERIES
8 worshipful duets by Phillip Keveren: As the Deer • Awesome God • Give Thanks • Great Is the Lord • Lord, I Lift Your Name on High • Shout to the Lord • There Is a Redeemer • We Fall Down.
00311203 Piano Duet $11.95

Shout to the Lord!
THE PHILLIP KEVEREN SERIES
14 favorite praise songs, including: As the Deer • El Shaddai • Give Thanks • Great Is the Lord • How Beautiful • More Precious Than Silver • Oh Lord, You're Beautiful • A Shield About Me • Shine, Jesus, Shine • Shout to the Lord • Thy Word • and more.
00310699 Piano Solo $12.95

The Chris Tomlin Collection
15 songs from one of the leading artists and composers in Contemporary Christian music, including the favorites: Be Glorified • Holy Is the Lord • How Can I Keep from Singing • How Great Is Our God • Indescribable • Not to Us • Take My Life • We Fall Down • and more.
00306951 P/V/G $16.95

Worship Songs & Stories
Text by Lindsay Terry
This collection features PVG music plus the inspiring and intriguing stories behind 20 beloved praise & worship songs. Includes: Blessed Be Your Name • Days of Elijah • Forever • God of Wonders • He Is Exalted • Holy Is the Lord • I Stand in Awe • There Is None Like You • We Fall Down • and more.
00311478 P/V/G $14.95

Worship – The Ultimate Collection
Matching folio with 24 top worship favorites, including: Blessed Be Your Name • Draw Me Close • God of Wonders • He Reigns • Here I Am to Worship • I Could Sing of Your Love Forever • Lord, Reign in Me • Open the Eyes of My Heart • Yesterday, Today and Forever • and more.
00313337 P/V/G $17.95

Worship Together Piano Solo Favorites
A dozen great worship songs tastefully arranged for intermediate piano solo. Includes: Amazing Grace (My Chains Are Gone) • Beautiful Savior (All My Days) • Facedown • The Heart of Worship • How Great Is Our God • and more.
00311477 Piano Solo.................................$12.95

Worship Without Words
arr. Ken Medema
The highly creative Ken Medema has arranged 13 worship songs and classic hymns, perfect for blended worship. Includes: As the Deer • I Could Sing of Your Love Forever • Open the Eyes of My Heart • You Are My All in All • and more.
00311229 Piano Solo.................................$12.95

The Most Romantic Music In The World

Arranged for piano, voice, and guitar

The Best Love Songs Ever - 2nd Edition

This revised edition includes 65 romantic favorites: Always • Beautiful in My Eyes • Can You Feel the Love Tonight • Endless Love • Have I Told You Lately • Misty • Something • Through the Years • Truly • When I Fall in Love • and more.

00359198 ....$19.95

The Big Book of Love Songs - 2nd Edition

80 romantic hits in many musical styles: Always on My Mind • Cherish • Fields of Gold • I Honestly Love You • I'll Be There • Isn't It Romantic? • Lady • My Heart Will Go On • Save the Best for Last • Truly • Wonderful Tonight • and more.

00310784 ....$19.95

The Christian Wedding Songbook

37 songs of love and commitment, including: Bonded Together • Cherish the Treasure • Flesh of My Flesh • Go There with You • Household of Faith • How Beautiful • I Will Be Here • Love Will Be Our Home • Make Us One • Parent's Prayer • This Is the Day • This Very Day • and more.

00310681 ....$16.95

The Bride's Guide to Wedding Music

This great guide is a complete resource for planning wedding music. It includes a thorough article on choosing music for a wedding ceremony, and 65 songs in many different styles to satisfy lots of different tastes. The songs are grouped by categories, including preludes, processionals, recessionals, traditional sacred songs, popular songs, country songs, contemporary Christian songs, Broadway numbers, and new age piano music.

00310615 ....$19.95

Broadway Love Songs

50 romantic favorites from shows such as *Phantom of the Opera, Guys and Dolls, Oklahoma!, South Pacific, Fiddler on the Roof* and more. Songs include: All I Ask of You • Bewitched • I've Grown Accustomed to Her Face • Love Changes Everything • So in Love • Sunrise, Sunset • Unexpected Song • We Kiss in a Shadow • and more.

00311558 ....$15.95

Country Love Songs - 4th Edition

This edition features 34 romantic country favorites: Amazed • Breathe • Could I Have This Dance • Forever and Ever, Amen • I Need You • The Keeper of the Stars • Love Can Build a Bridge • One Boy, One Girl • Stand by Me • This Kiss • Through the Years • Valentine • You Needed Me • more.

00311528 ....$14.95

The Definitive Love Collection - 2nd Edition

100 romantic favorites – all in one convenient collection! Includes: All I Ask of You • Can't Help Falling in Love • Endless Love • The Glory of Love • Have I Told You Lately • Heart and Soul • Lady in Red • Love Me Tender • My Romance • So in Love • Somewhere Out There • Unforgettable • Up Where We Belong • When I Fall in Love • and more!

00311681 ....$24.95

I Will Be Here

Over two dozen romantic selections from top contemporary Christian artists such as Susan Ashton, Avalon, Steven Curtis Chapman, Twila Paris, Sonicflood, and others. Songs include: Answered Prayer • Beautiful in My Eyes • Celebrate You • For Always • Give Me Forever (I Do) • Go There with You • How Beautiful • Love Will Be Our Home • and more.

00306472 ....$17.95

Love Songs
Budget Books Series

74 favorite love songs, including: And I Love Her • Cherish • Crazy • Endless Love • Fields of Gold • I Just Called to Say I Love You • I'll Be There • (You Make Me Feel Like) A Natural Woman • Wonderful Tonight • You Are So Beautiful • and more.

00310834 ....$12.95

The New Complete Wedding Songbook

41 of the most requested and beloved songs for romance and weddings: Anniversary Song • Ave Maria • Canon in D (Pachelbel) • Could I Have This Dance • Endless Love • I Love You Truly • Just the Way You Are • The Lord's Prayer • Through the Years • You Needed Me • Your Song • and more.

00309326 ....$12.95

New Ultimate Love and Wedding Songbook

This whopping songbook features 90 songs of devotion, including: The Anniversary Waltz • Can't Smile Without You • Could I Have This Dance • Endless Love • For All We Know • Forever and Ever, Amen • The Hawaiian Wedding Song • Here, There and Everywhere • I Only Have Eyes for You • Just the Way You Are • Longer • The Lord's Prayer • Love Me Tender • Misty • Somewhere • Sunrise, Sunset • Through the Years • Trumpet Voluntary • Your Song • and more.

00361445 ....$19.95

Romance - Boleros Favoritos

Features 48 Spanish and Latin American favorites: Aquellos Ojos Verdes • Bésame Mucho • El Reloj • Frenes • Inolvidable • La Vida Es Un Sueño • Perfidia • Siempre En Mi Corazón • Solamente Una Vez • more.

00310383 ....$16.95

Soulful Love Songs

Features 35 favorite romantic ballads, including: All My Life • Baby, Come to Me • Being with You • Endless Love • Hero • I Just Called to Say I Love You • I'll Make Love to You • I'm Still in Love with You • Killing Me Softly with His Song • My Cherie Amour • My Eyes Adored You • Oh Girl • On the Wings of Love • Overjoyed • Tonight, I Celebrate My Love • Vision of Love • You Are the Sunshine of My Life • You've Made Me So Very Happy • and more.

00310922 ....$14.95

Selections from
VH1's 100 Greatest Love Songs

Nearly 100 love songs chosen for their emotion. Includes: Always on My Mind • Baby, I Love Your Way • Careless Whisper • Endless Love • How Deep Is Your Love • I Got You Babe • If You Leave Me Now • Love Me Tender • My Heart Will Go On • Unchained Melody • You're Still the One • and dozens more!

00306506 ....$27.95

1004